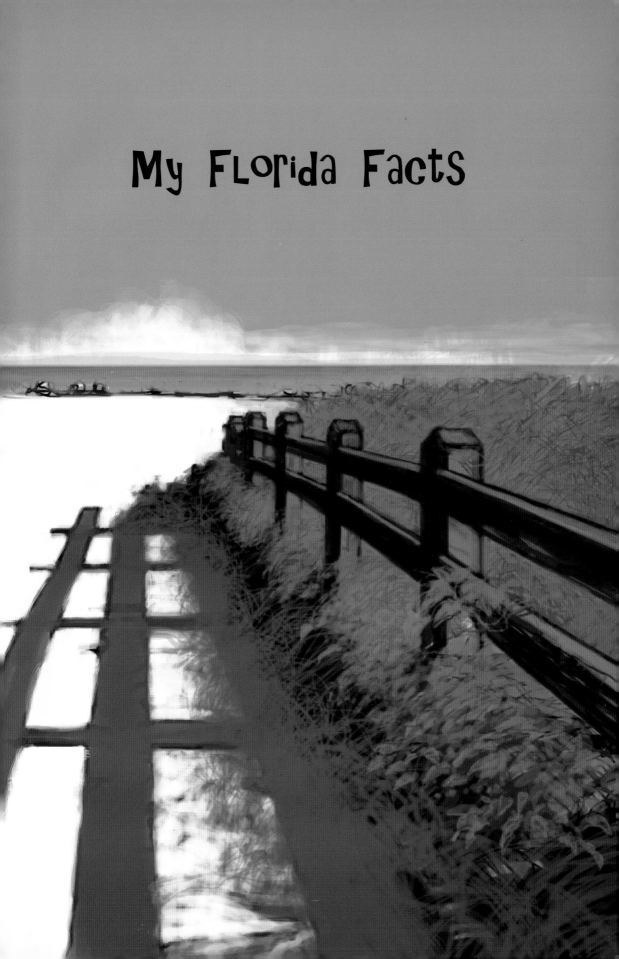

My Florida Facts

My Florida Facts

Russell W. Johnson and Annie P. Johnson

Illustrations by Michael Swing

Pineapple Press, Inc.
Sarasota, Florida

We dedicate this book to the many students across the Sunshine State who are required to learn Florida state facts, but prefer to . . . *sing them instead.*

Inquiries should be addressed to:

Pineapple Press, Inc.
P.O. Box 3889
Sarasota, Florida 34230

www.pineapplepress.com

Library of Congress Cataloging-in-Publication Data

Johnson, Russell W., 1958-
My Florida facts / Russell W. Johnson and Annie P. Johnson ; illustrations by Michael Swing. -- 1st ed.
    p. cm.
ISBN 978-1-56164-430-8 (hb : alk. paper)
1. Florida--Juvenile literature. I. Johnson, Annie, 1942- II. Swing, Michael, ill. III. Title.
F311.3.J65 2009
975.9--dc22

                    2008045326

First Edition
10 9 8 7 6 5 4 3 2 1

Design by Shé Hicks
Printed in China

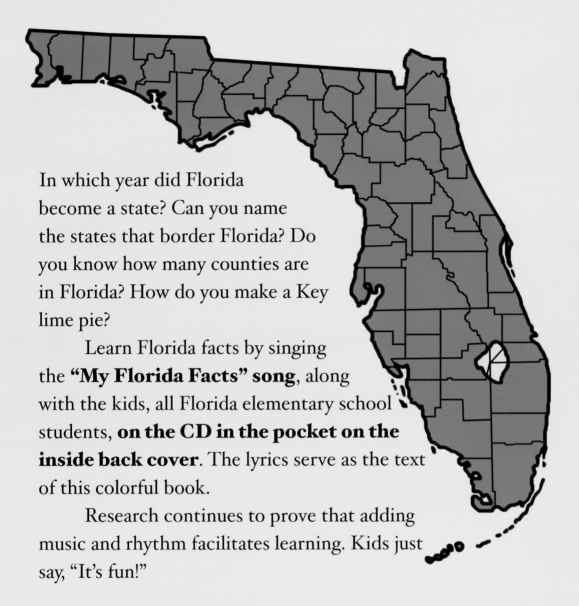

In which year did Florida become a state? Can you name the states that border Florida? Do you know how many counties are in Florida? How do you make a Key lime pie?

Learn Florida facts by singing the **"My Florida Facts" song**, along with the kids, all Florida elementary school students, **on the CD in the pocket on the inside back cover**. The lyrics serve as the text of this colorful book.

Research continues to prove that adding music and rhythm facilitates learning. Kids just say, "It's fun!"

My Florida Facts

* CHORUS: Florida's a great state, as all of you must know.
                  It does me good to feel the flow of white sand
                     through my toes.
                  I swim and fish and lounge around beneath the
                     tropic sun.
                  But there are facts that I must learn, so I can
                     teach someone.

The "Sunshine State" is our nickname, the sabal palm our
    tree.
The capital of Florida is . . . Tallahassee.
We became the 27th state in 1845.
The climate and the scenery make me glad that I'm alive.

Florida's Cape Canaveral put the first man on the moon.
Our feathered friend the mockingbird can carry quite a tune.
In warmer waters you will find the peaceful manatee.
With miles and miles of citrus groves, your health is
    guaranteed, oh . . . (chorus)*

I'm sure you've heard this Florida song: it's "Way Down
    Upon the Suwannee River"
Where the 'gators and them sneaky snakes can give you quite
    a shiver.
Old folks like our climate and often come to stay
While young folks on vacation come prepared to play.

67 counties and many famous springs,
From Florida's Panhandle to Key West you'll see things
Like St. Augustine, the oldest city in the U.S.A.,
And Lake Okeechobee, it's the biggest in the state.

Alabama and Georgia are our neighbors, don't cha know.
Our shores border the Atlantic and the Gulf of Mexico.
Come visit, enjoy, but . . . just remember:
Hurricanes can blow from June through November . . .
　　(chorus)*

I'd like to spend more time with you and sing about the
　　Keys,
Amusement parks, coral reefs, and sailin' with the breeze.
I've shared with you some "Florida Facts" but now must
　　say goodbye.
It seems I've got a cravin' for a piece of Key lime pie —
Our famous Key lime pie . . . (mmmmmmmm,
　　mmmmmmm)

Written by Russell Johnson (inspired by Annie)
© 1998

UNITED STATES

The "Sunshine State" is our nickname,

FLORIDA

the sabal palm our tree.

The capital of Florida is . . . Tallahassee.

FLORIDA

TALLAHASSEE

Florida State
Capitol Complex
at Nighttime

1. Delaware
2. Pennsylvania
3. New Jersey
4. Georgia
5. Connecticut
6. Massachusetts
7. Maryland
8. South Carolina
9. New Hampshire
10. Virginia
11. New York
12. North Carolina
13. Rhode Island
14. Vermont
15. Kentucky
16. Tennessee
17. Ohio
18. Louisiana
19. Indiana
20. Mississippi
21. Illinois
22. Alabama
23. Maine
24. Missouri
25. Arkansas
26. Michigan

27. Florida

1845

We became the 27th state in 1845.

The climate and the scenery
make me glad that I'm alive.

CAPE
CANAVERAL
Florida

Florida's Cape Canaveral put the
first man on the moon.

Our feathered friend the mockingbird
can carry quite a tune.

In warmer waters you
will find the peaceful manatee.

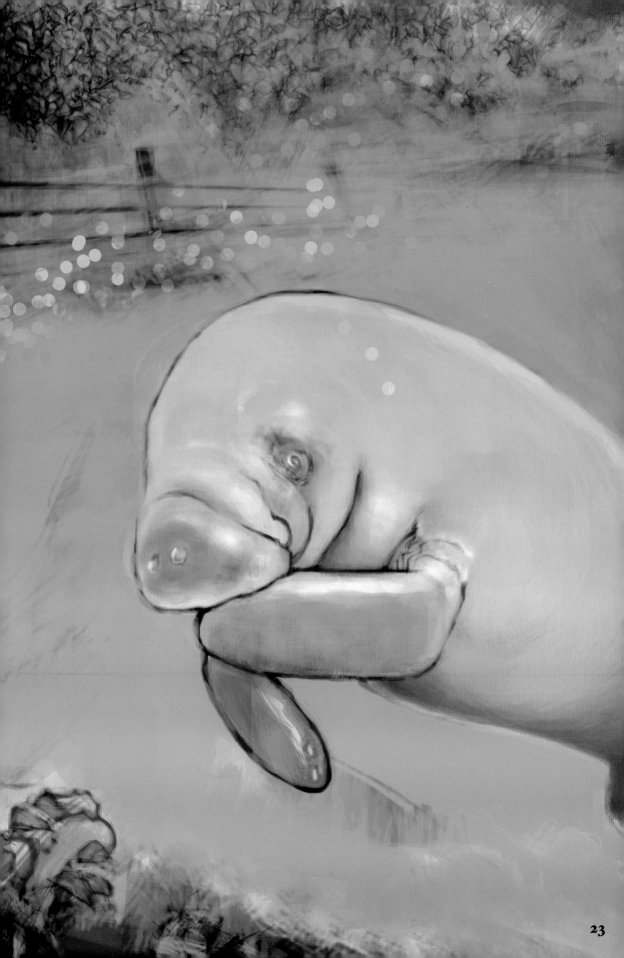

With miles and miles of citrus groves,
your health is guaranteed, oh . . .

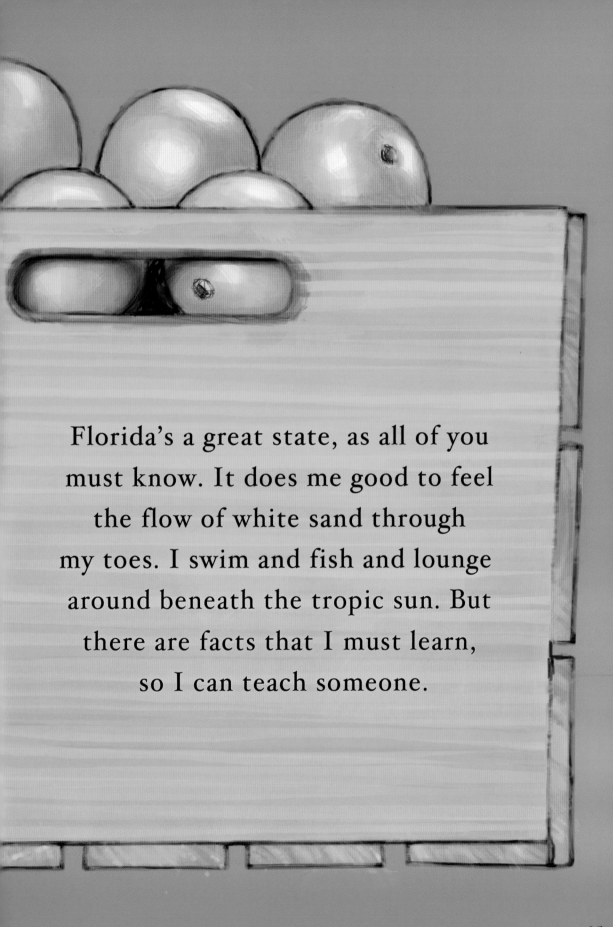

Florida's a great state, as all of you
must know. It does me good to feel
the flow of white sand through
my toes. I swim and fish and lounge
around beneath the tropic sun. But
there are facts that I must learn,
so I can teach someone.

I'm sure you've heard this Florida song:
it's "Way Down Upon the Suwannee River"

26

Where the 'gators

and them sneaky snakes

can give you quite a shiver.

Old folks like our climate
and often come to stay

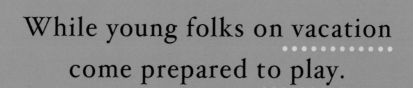

While young folks on vacation
come prepared to play.

1. Escambia	24. Gilchrist	47. Seminole
2. Santa Rosa	25. Columbia	48. Manatee
3. Okaloosa	26. Alachua	49. Hardee
4. Walton	27. Union	50. DeSoto
5. Holmes	28. Baker	51. Highlands
6. Washington	29. Bradford	52. Osceola
7. Jackson	30. Clay	53. Brevard
8. Bay	31. Duval	54. Sarasota
9. Calhoun	32. Nassau	55. Charlotte
10. Gulf	33. Marion	56. Glades
11. Liberty	34. Putnam	57. Okeechobee
12. Gadsden	35. St. Johns	58. Indian River
13. Franklin	36. Citrus	59. Lee
14. Wakulla	37. Sumter	60. Hendry
15. Leon	38. Lake	61. Palm Beach
16. Jefferson	39. Volusia	62. Martin
17. Taylor	40. Flagler	63. St. Lucie
18. Madison	41. Hernando	64. Collier
19. Dixie	42. Pasco	65. Broward
20. Lafayette	43. Pinellas	66. Monroe
21. Suwannee	44. Hillsborough	67. Mami-Dade
22. Hamilton	45. Polk	
23. Levy	46. Orange	

67 counties

2 15 16 18 22 32
14 17 21 25 28 31
20 27 30 35
19 24 29 26 34 40
23 33 39
36 47
37 38 46
41
42 52 53
43 44 45 58
48 49 57 63
51
54 50 62
55 56 61
59 60
65
64
66 67

67

and many famous springs,

PANHANDLE

From Florida's Panhandle

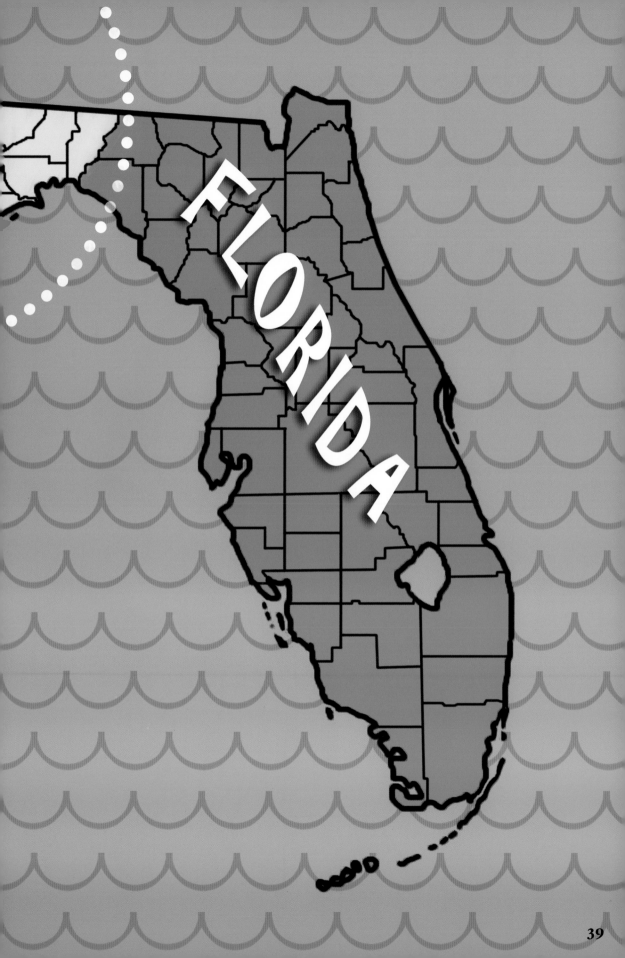

FLORIDA

to Key West you'll see things

FLORIDA KEYS

KEY WEST

SOUTHERNMOST
POINT
CONTINENTAL
U.S.A.

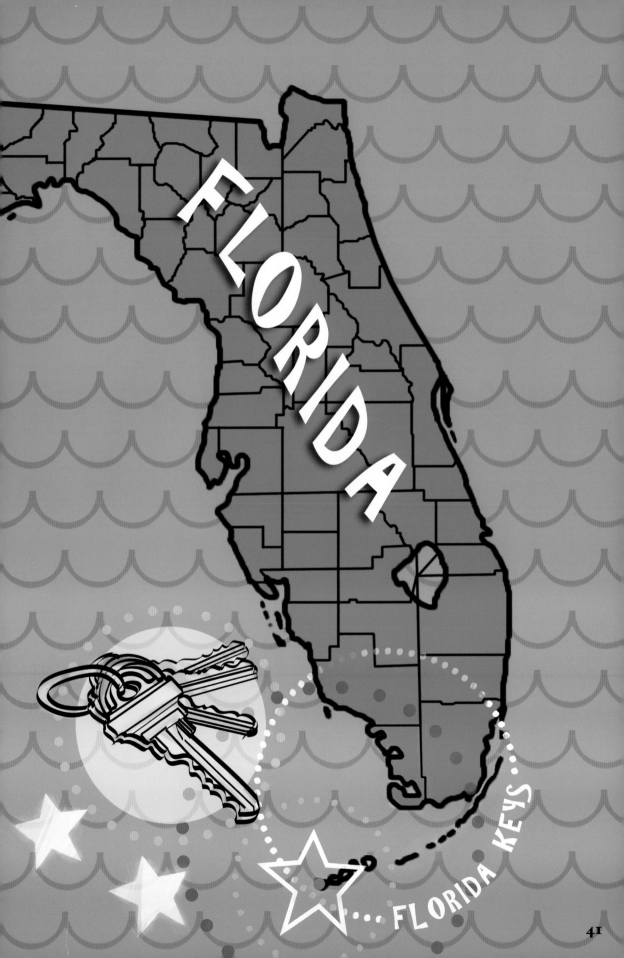

FLORIDA

FLORIDA KEYS

St. Augustine

Castillo de
San Marcos
1672
First Stone
Fortress

Founded 1565

Like St. Augustine,
the oldest city in the U.S.A.,

RoSeate SpooNbiLLS

And Lake Okeechobee,
it's the biggest in the state.

LAKE OKEECHOBEE

Second-Largest
Freshwater Lake
in U.S.A.

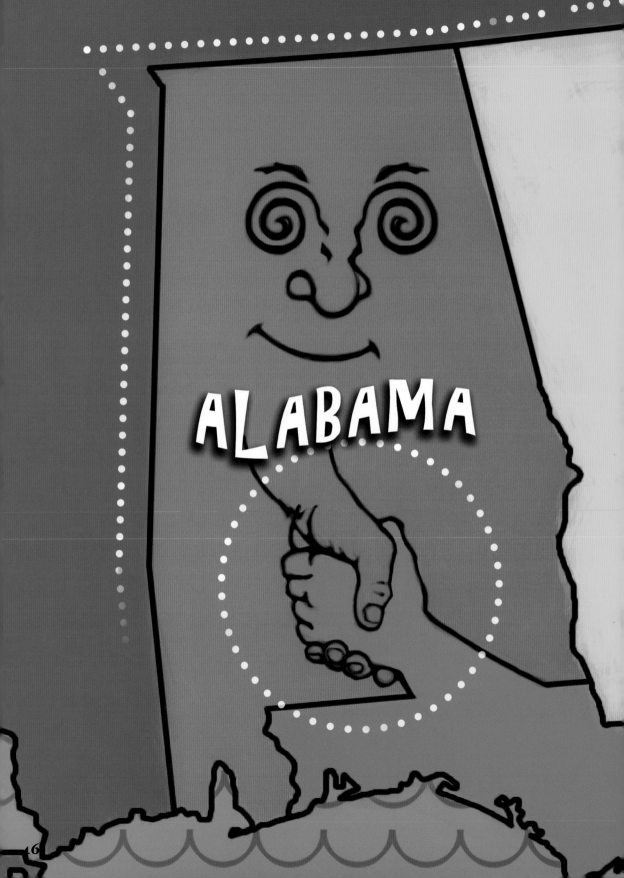

Alabama and Georgia are our neighbors,
don't cha know.

GEORGIA

FLORIDA

UNITED STATES

GULF OF

MEXICO

ATLANTIC

FLORIDA

MEXICO

CUBA

Our shores border the Atlantic
and the Gulf of Mexico.

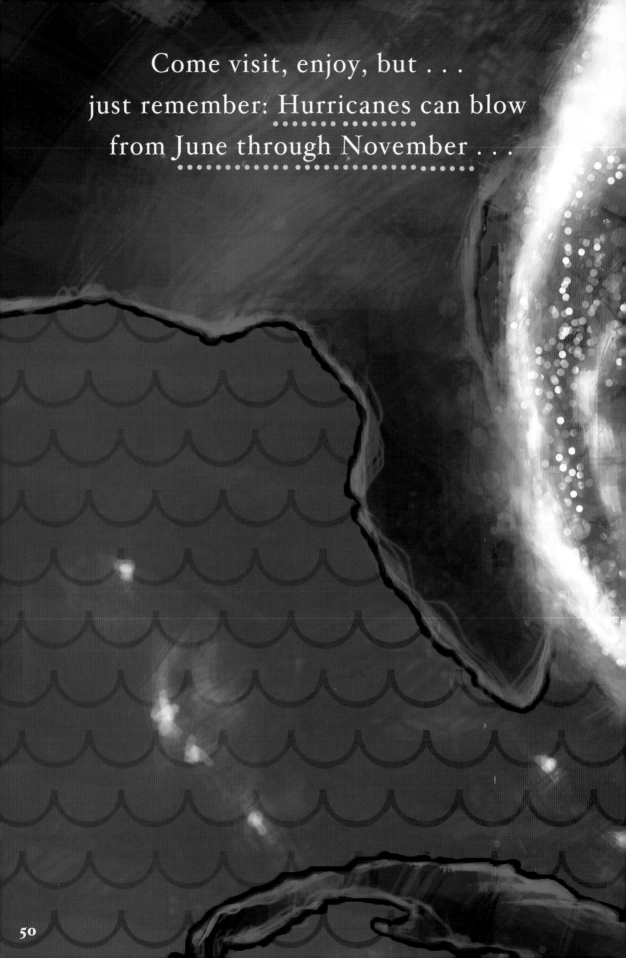

Come visit, enjoy, but . . .
just remember: Hurricanes can blow
from June through November . . .

50

Florida's a great state, as all of you must know. It does me good to feel the flow of white sand through my toes. I swim and fish and lounge around beneath the tropic sun. But there are facts that I must learn, so I can teach someone.

I'd like to spend more time with you
and sing about the Keys,

Amusement parks,

coral reefs,

and sailin'   with the breeze.

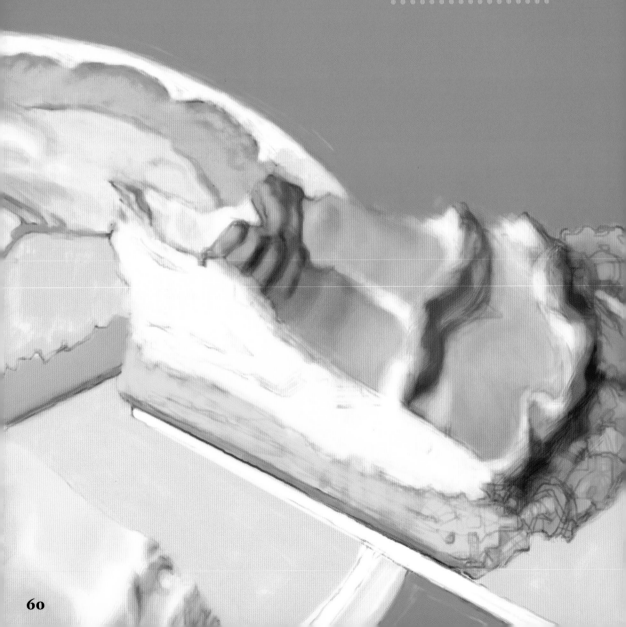

I've shared with you some "Florida Facts"
but now must say goodbye.
It seems I've got a cravin'
for a piece of Key lime pie~

KEY LIME PIE RECIPE

1 (14 oz.) can sweetened condensed milk

4 egg yolks

4 oz. Florida Key West Key Lime Juice

9" graham cracker pie crust

Mix milk and egg yolks completely with electric mixer.
Slowly add Key lime juice and mix thoroughly. Pour
into 9-inch prepared graham cracker pie shell.

For meringue topping, bake at 350° for 8 minutes.
Place meringue on hot pie, sealing edges to crust, and
toast in oven to a golden brown. Keep a close eye on it.
It will start to toast very fast. Let pie cool and put in
refrigerator.

For whipped topping, bake at 350° for 10 minutes.
Let pie cool and put in refrigerator. Spread whipped
topping on pie before serving.

Our famous Key lime pie . . .
(mmmmmmm, mmmmmmm)

Russ and Annie Johnson have been teaching children in early grades for over twenty years, always using music and movement to enhance learning. They now teach in St. Augustine, Florida, and present workshops nationwide. Their website is www.bldgfoundations.com.

Here are some other books from Pineapple Press on related topics. For a complete catalog, write to Pineapple Press, P.O. Box 3889, Sarasota, Florida 34230-3889, or call (800) 746-3275. Or visit our website at www.pineapplepress.com.

My Florida Alphabet by Russell W. Johnson and Annie P. Johnson, illustrated by John Hume. Join Big Al, the tugboat, as he chugs through Florida from A to Z. Sing along, performing the gestures for each letter. Includes a CD with the easily learned song, performed by children. Ages 4–8. (hb)

Florida A to Z by Susan Jane Ryan, illustrated by Carol Tornatore. From Alligator to Zephyrhills, you'll find more information on Florida packed in this alphabet than you can imagine—almost 200 facts about Florida personalities, history, geography, nature, and culture. Full-color throughout. Ages 9–12. (hb)

Those Amazing Animals series. Written by various authors, each book in the series offers 20 questions and answers with color pictures and funny illustrations sure to engage children and teach them about animals such as alligators, owls, turtles, eagles, pelicans, butterflies, manatees, dolphins, flamingos, vultures, and lizards. Includes fun activities to make and do. Ages 5–9. (hb, pb)

America's REAL First Thanksgiving by Robyn Gioia. When most Americans think of the first Thanksgiving, they think of the Pilgrims and the Indians in New England in 1621. But on September 8, 1565, the Spanish and the native Timucua celebrated with a feast of thanksgiving in St. Augustine. Teacher's activity guide available. Ages 9–14. (hb, pb)

Everglades: An Ecosystem Facing Choices and Challenges by Anne E. Ake. The Everglades is like no other place in the world. Its shallow, slowly flowing waters create an ecosystem of mysterious beauty with a great diversity of plant and animal life. But the Everglades ecosystem is in trouble. Learn about how the Comprehensive Restoration Plan (CERP), the largest restoration plan ever undertaken, is bringing many groups together to try to save the Everglades and south Florida. Lots of color photos. Ages 11–14. (hb)

The Young Naturalist's Guide to Florida, 2nd Edition by Peggy Sias Lantz and Wendy A. Hale. Provides up-to-date information about Florida's wonderful natural places and the plants and creatures that live here—many of which are found nowhere else in the United States. Learn about careers in the environmental field and how to help protect Florida's beautiful places. Ages 10–14. (pb)

Florida Lighthouses for Kids by Elinor De Wire. Learn why some lighthouses are tall and some short, why a cat parachuted off St. Augustine Lighthouse, and much more. Lots of color pictures. Ages 9 and up. (pb)

The Florida Quiz Book: How Much Do You Know about Florida? by Hollee Temple. Over 2500 questions and answers on topics like Agriculture, Architecture, Art, the Economy, Ecosystems, the Environment, Plants, Animals, Geology, Geography, History, the Keys, Law, Literature, Meteorology, the Oceans and Coastline, Parks, Space Science, and good old general Florida Statistics. (pb)

Native Americans in Florida by Kevin M. McCarthy. Long before the first European explorers set foot on Florida soil, numerous Native American tribes hunted, honored their gods, and built burial mounds. This book explores the importance of preserving the past and how archaeologists do their work. Ages 10 and up. (hb)

African Americans in Florida by Maxine D. Jones and Kevin McCarthy. Profiles more than fifty African Americans during four centuries of Florida history. Traces the role of African Americans played in his discovery, exploration, and settlement of Florida as well as through the Civil War to the Civil Rights movement. Ages 10 and up. (pb)

Legends of the Seminoles by Betty Mae Jumper with Peter Gallagher, paintings by Guy LaBree. For the first time, stories and legends handed down through generations by tribal elders have been set down for all to enjoy. Each tale is illustrated with an original color painting. (hb, pb)